POETIC VOYAGES
MILTON KEYNES

Edited by Donna Samworth

First published in Great Britain in 2001 by
YOUNG WRITERS
Remus House,
Coltsfoot Drive,
Peterborough, PE2 9JX
Telephone (01733) 890066

HB ISBN 0 75433 172 5
SB ISBN 0 75433 173 3

FOREWORD

Young Writers was established in 1991 with the aim
to promote creative writing in children, to make
reading and writing poetry fun.

This year once again, proved to be a tremendous
success with over 88,000 entries received nationwide.

The Poetic Voyages competition has shown us the
high standard of work and effort that children are
capable of today. It is a reflection of the teaching
skills in schools, the enthusiasm and creativity they
have injected into their pupils shines clearly within
this anthology.

The task of selecting poems was therefore a difficult
one but nevertheless, an enjoyable experience. We
hope you are as pleased with the final selection in
Poetic Voyages Milton Keynes as we are.

CONTENTS

The Poems

PERFECT CHRISTMAS ... NOT!

Christmas is cancelled,
It's terribly sad,
Santa's been grounded!
For being so bad!
No more presents under the tree,
No more toys, oh dear, dear me!
Stocking's empty,
Sadness?
Plenty.
So Santa next year,
Bring us toys,
Be a dear!

Aisha Dickins (9)
Bradwell Village Middle School

I MET AT DARK THE KING OF NIGHT

I met at dark the king of night,
His was a bewitching gloomy face.
Through undisturbed cemeteries and eternal subways,
Darkening every little place.

His cloak was black of shadows,
An inky crown upon his head,
Incinerated like charcoal,
Putting everything to sleep.

His night-time walk of quiet,
Through the hushed, soundless valley,
Gliding through trees and bushes,
Animals coming to comfort him.

The king's house up in the galaxy,
A luminous speck.
Which disappears in the sun's rays,
And comes back when dusk falls.

His chariot races around the world,
Chalking everything black.
Like a sheet, a blanket,
Making owls hoot with glee.

I met at dark the king of night,
His was a bewitching, gloomy face.
Through undisturbed cemeteries and eternal subways,
Darkening every little place.

Fiona Maguire (11)
Bradwell Village Middle School

MY GRAN

My gran is as short as a child.
Her hair is like a matted ball of grey fur.
Her eyes are like big rounded snowballs
With little stars of blue.
Her face is like a furry peach.
When she walks she is like a slow,
Newborn rabbit.
When she sits she is like a crooked twig.
When she laughs she is like a croaky frog.
When she sleeps she is like a roly-poly bear.
The best thing about my gran is, she is kind
And she always gives me biscuits!

Alicia Perkins (8)
Bradwell Village Middle School

I HEAR

When I think of my PlayStation
I hear . . .
The click of the lid closing, and the
Push of a button.
The sounds of the controls rattling
In the hands of a child.
The screaming as a monster appears,
Or the sound of victory as you win a battle.
Digital sounds of lasers and motor cars.
The bellowing shout *'turn it down'*
Then arguing, like ravens, over who has what.
The footsteps of someone coming.
And then click and 'owwwhh!' as
The controls are taken.
And there is the quiet pitter-patter of
Rain as the silent flick of a book is heard.

Daniel Alder (12)
Bradwell Village Middle School

WHEN I WAS 8 YEARS OLD

I loved the Simpson's yellow skin,
The monsters of Pokémon,
The masters of Digimon too,
The quiz The Weakest Link
And the channel of Sky One.

The smell of hot dogs,
The taste of burgers,
The fish of fish fingers.
The crunchiness of chicken nuggets,
The twirls of Twizzlers.

The sun of Majorca,
The beach of Cornwall,
The hard languages of Japan and Rome,
And the clubs of 'Wild Duck.'

The fizziness of cola,
The warm cup of tea,
The coldness of 'lemon and blackcurrant,'
The taste of water,

The delicious taste of milk.
The monsters on 'Pokémon The Movie,'
The toys of 'Toy Story 2,'
The reptiles of 'Dinosaur,'
And the Bond films of 007 and 'Octopus.'

Lee Gardner (8)
Bradwell Village Middle School

CHRISTMAS TREE LIGHTS

Flashing, sparkling
Brightly coloured
Christmas tree lights

Each little light
Brightens the night
The tree's best thing

They feel jolly
And it feels bright
As they flash

Sherri Jay (10)
Bradwell Village Middle School

THE RIVER'S JOURNEY

The mountainous, rocky stream,
Bubbles gently and,
Trickles effortlessly,
Like a running tap.

As the dribbling stream grows when it flows,
It becomes lively and,
It twists and turns
Like a wriggling worm.

The bumpy stream comes to the end,
It falls powerfully and,
It splashes with a crash
Like a shower just being turned on.

As the sparkling stream is now a river,
It gracefully glides to its end and,
It stretches smoothly,
Like an elastic band.

The river is now in the expanded ocean,
It laps into massive waves, and,
It rushes happily to its freedom,
Like a trapped bird escaping from its cage.

Sinead Kerslake (10)
Holne Chase Combined School

SOMEWHERE IN A SCHOOL

A large group of hysterical children are
Making one hell of a racket.
With their wide open mouths.

The exhausted teacher collapses
On a chair in the small staffroom

Disgraceful children are jumping
And rolling around in the
Soggy wet mud in the playground.

The terrified head teacher gallops
Into his office while the cheeky
Children throw food at him.

Hannah Devoil (10)
Holne Chase Combined School

THE RIVER'S JOURNEY

The flowing, rocky stream,
Bubbles gently and,
Sprinkles calmly,
Like a witch's cauldron.

The running, expanding stream,
Splashes rapidly and,
Dribbles wildly,
Like a child dreaming of chocolate.

The battling, twisting waterfall,
Struggles helplessly while it,
Crashes frighteningly,
Like a thunderous storm.

The twirling waterfall calms down,
Drifting slowly and,
Bouncing gracefully,
Like an advanced ballet dancer doing a split leap.

The stretching sea,
Sways relaxingly and,
Laps softly,
Like a choir of angels singing a Christmas carol.

Amelia Cudmore (9)
Holne Chase Combined School

MY VISION

My vision of the future,
Very far away from here,
They'll have giant, iron robots,
With super noses, eyes and ears.

People using super powers,
Plants that grow with wacky hair,
I think I'll really like it,
When we finally get there.

My vision of the future,
Quite a bit of time from now,
Can't wait to get there gee whiz wow!
They'll have supersonic lasers
That can blow up anything,
They'll have new discovered
Animals like chimpanzees that sing.

They'll have 'bits and bobs'
And thingamajigs that we have never seen,
In fact it's so good I think I'll build a time machine.

Andrew Thomas Bond (9)
Holne Chase Combined School

SOMEWHERE IN THE WORLD TODAY. . .

A chaotic flock of multicoloured birds are being
Banished from their home as it is being chopped
Down thoughtlessly.

Intelligent gorillas are being captured disgustingly to
Be put in a prison where people stand and stare idiotically.

Zebras are being violently shot as inconsiderate
Hunters think of a rug of the zebra's beautiful skin
On his sparkling varnished floor.

Starving porcupines are rummaging through bushes
Hungrily because hunters are carelessly eating their food.

Colossal elephants with scaly wrinkled skin are
Being shot painfully for their wonderful cream
Treasured tusks.

A racing cheetah chases hungrily after his petrified
Prey as his stomach starts to rumble like an earthquake.

Alix Kelly (9)
Holne Chase Combined School

NAMES

A is for Ann, who eats apples,
B is for Ben, who rings bells,
C is for Craig, who crawls,
D is for David, who rides donkeys,
E is for Elle, who loves elephants,
F is for Frazer, who likes feathers,
G is for Gary, who loves golf,
H is for Harry, who hates hamsters,
I is for Izzy, who has iguanas,
J is for Jason, who squashes jelly,
K is for Katie, who fly's kites,
L is for Lucy, who drinks lots of lime,
M is for Matthew, who eats marshmallows,
N is for Natalie who eats nuts
O is for Oliver, who adores owls,
P is for Peter, who loves peas,
Q is for the Queen, who eats quail,
R is for Robert, who likes lions roaring,
S is for Stacey, who loves snow,
T is for Tom, who teases Tim,
U is for Ursula, who loves unicorns,
V is for Vanessa, who likes vixens,
W is for William, who collects worms,
X is for Xavier, who hates X-rays,
Y is for Yvonne, who loves her yacht,
Z is for Zack, who keeps zebras.

Ben Hammond (9)
Holne Chase Combined School

OBJECTS

A is for Alice, who ate lots of ants.
B is for Bertha, who bit Ben's bum.
C is for Cuthbert, who likes cakes and corn.
D is for Denis, who can divide well.
E is for Elma the elephant.
F is for Fred, who lies in his bed.
G is for George, who gnaws and grunts.
H is for Hercules, who hums and sings.
I is for I am ignorant.
J is for Jo, who gives joy.
K is for Karen, who wills Ken.
L is for Laura, who rules the land.
M is for Martha the monkey.
N is for Norman the Norwegian
O is for Olive the orange.
P is for Percy the panda.
Q is for Queenie the queen.
R is for Rebecca the rabbit.
S is for Sidney the snake.
T is for Tiffany that likes tea.
U is for Ursula the orang-utan
V is for Vickie Vulture.
W is for William the worm
X is for Xena X-ray.
Y is for Yvonne Yo-yo.
Z is for Zena zebra.

Jo Hayes (7)
Holne Chase Combined School

COLIN BEAR PULLS GIRLS' HAIR!

There was a young man named Colin Bear who liked to pull girls' hair.
Now one day the person named Colin Bear.
Went up to his teacher and pulled his teacher's mask that had a snout.
Then the teacher went up to Colin Bear and pulled his head off
          And he could not do anything about it.

Then the doctor phoned and said.
'This is the end of his days.'

Sam Ive (8)
Holne Chase Combined School

WINTER'S COMING

Winter's coming round the corner
Autumn's been and gone
The rain and snow is coming back
The leaves fall with ease
I look forward to the days of snow
Where everything turns white
The dull days of autumn have
Been in the past.

The snowball fights are drawing closer
No more warm nights
Then the rain comes back again
And washes the snow away
We sit in bed and hope for snow
The white stuff to fall
Then days and days later
It falls and falls again

After weeks it goes again and
The dull days are back
Another week 'til Christmas
The joy of all time
The presents, the laughter
The happiness too
The family gathers for the joyful time.

Claire Maley (11)
Holne Chase Combined School

MY CROCODILE

He stays in ditches forever and ever
His skin feels like rubber leather,
And is sly but very clever.

He's going to get a child tomorrow,
Bewares he's out to follow,
Some parents will be full of sorrow.

Where he lives is steep,
But could also be deep,
And remember he's a creep,

Imagine you are in his tummy,
He would think you are yummy,
So if he dares beware, beware!

Crystal Edwards (9)
Holne Chase Combined School

THE RIVER'S JOURNEY

The mountain's rocky stream
Bubbles gently,
Trickles calmly
Like a running tap

The bigger sweeping river
Twirling and swirling like a worm,
Thundering hard
Like a hurricane

The enormous waterfall
Sweeps down,
Thundering powerfully
Like an earthquake

The big river
Drifting slowly,
Calmly slowing down
Like a witch's cauldron

Keiron Hayes (10)
Holne Chase Combined School

SOMEWHERE UNDER THE OCEAN

Somewhere under the ocean, there's hundreds
Of bright scaled fish swimming quickly around.

Somewhere under the ocean, there's dangerous
Silver sharks swimming quickly around.

Somewhere under the ocean, there's scuba-divers
Taking photos of all the wonderful wildlife around.

Somewhere under the ocean there's many colourful
Plants swishing and splashing around.

Somewhere on the top of the ocean, there's a big boat
With me on it, watching the busy sea life and wobbling around.

Nicola Bird (10)
Holne Chase Combined School

CATS

Adventurous cats
Bloodsucking cats
Cool cats
Dribbling cats
Embarrassed cats
Floppy cats
Gentle cats
Heartbroken cats
Indigo cats
Jolly cats
King cats
Loving cats
Muddy cats
Nutty cats
Outrageous cats
Pale cats
Quiet cats
Rolling cats
Stray cats
Travelling cats
Upside down cats
Violent cats
Working cats
X-raying cats
Young cats
Zapping cats

Sarah Esau (9)
Holne Chase Combined School

ALPHABETICAL HABITS

A is for Amy, who always eats apples
B is for Becky, who has beaded braids in her hair
C is for Chris, who cracks crates
D is for Daniel, who dumps girls
E is for Emily, who eats eggy egg sandwiches
F is for Fred, who fights four-year-olds
G is for Gertie, who does Great Grandma's gardens
H is for Harry who hits big boys
I is for Indigo who fakes feeling ill
J is for Jack, who jumps, jumps
K is for Katie, who kills the king
L is for Lucy, who likes licking lollies
M is for Matthew, who munches mouldy eggs
N is for Naomi, who knits new hats
O is for Olive, who opens other people's presents
P is for Percy, who picks people's things
Q is for Quentin, who is very queer
R is for Rebecca who rips wrapping paper
S is for Sam, who slurps strange drinks
T is for Thomas, who takes Tic Tacs
U is for Una, who quits cool things
V is for Vincent who is very vicious
W is for William, who whacks witches
X is for Xena, who has X-rays
Y is for Yellow, who is very young
Z is for Zebra, who likes to celebrate with zest.

Rebecca Carter (9)
Holne Chase Combined School

ANIMALS

Amy loves ants and ants love Amy,
Becky loves bees, but bees hate Becky
Catherine kills cats and wears them as hats,
Declan decks dinosaurs, dinosaurs deck Declan,
Ealing loves elephants, elephants trample on Ealing
Frog the log sat on the dog,
Giraffes eat green grass,
Hippo Glippo is a *hippie hippo*
Iguana who's an ignorant iguana,
Joey Jay sang today;
Kangaroo made a loo,
Llamas laugh like lemons,
Monkeys, monkeys like tumbling monkeys,
Nats nick Naomi's knickers,
Octopus occupies old ladies,
Peacocks poke pelicans,
Quail is a queen,
Rabbit rules the rainforest,
Seagulls, steal their sell,
Tigers take telephones,
Unicorns who always say, 'ugh!'
Vixen is a vain vixen,
Whale wipes wet patches
X-ray fish, X-rays other fish,
Yak always likes to whack,
Zebra likes Debra.

Kory Shouler (9)
Holne Chase Combined School

SOUNDS FUNNY

A is for Adam, who eats apples
B is for Bryan, who bit Betty's bum
C is for Charlotte, who likes to eat cream
D is for Darren, who eats through his day
E is for Estelle, she is an elephant
F is for Farrah, who is very funny
G is for Garath who likes to play with Garry
H is for Haley, who acts like a horse
I is for Ian, who is an ice cube
J is for Janet who is jealous
K is for Karen, who lives in a cart
L is for Levi, who likes to eat lollies
M is for Melanie, who fell in love with Mark
N is for Neil, who eats nuts
O is for Oliver who eats oranges
P is for Pam, who delivers the post
Q is for Queenie, who answers all the questions
R is for Rachel, who likes to race
S is for Sophie, who is always safe
T is for Tom, who lost his taste
U is for Ursula, who marches up the stairs
V is for Volo who loves vinegar
W is for William, who loves water
X is for Xereces, who loves X-rays
Y is for Yoske, who is young
Z is for Zak, who lives in the zoo.

Sophie Figg (8)
Holne Chase Combined School

SILLY HABITS

A is for Andy who is always eating apples
B is for Becky who loves reading books
C is for Ceri who loves clapping
D is for Daniel, who loves dancing
E is for Evelyn who loves Edward
F is for Freddy who loves flowers
G is for Gary, who loves garages
H is for Helena who loves hedges
I is for Ian who loves India
J is for Joe who loves jokes
K is for Kelly who loves kicking
L is for Lauren who loves leaping
M is for Michael who loves mixing cakes
N is for Nicci who loves knots
O is for Oliver who likes oranges
P is for Poppy who loves pepper
Q is for Queenie who likes quarters
R is for Rachel Ringing who loves her bells
S is for Sandra Selling who loves buying salt
T is for Tommy Tanger who loves Tic Tac
U is for Una Umbrella who loves the rain
V is for Venus Vaperate who loves fridges
W is for Wendy Windy who loves walls
X is for Mr. X-ray who loves light
Y is for Yeane Yellow who loves colours
Z is for Zeasus Zebra who loves animals.

Daniella Barden (9)
Holne Chase Combined School

ALPHABET NAMES AND HABITS

A is for Andrew who attacks beehives.
B is for Bradley who brings knives.
C is for Chris who catches fish.
D is for Daniel who dries a dish.
E is for Emma who eats lots of fish.
F is for Fred who feeds his dish.
G is for Gertrude who gobbles her food.
H is for Harry who hurries in the nude.
I is for Imran who introduces people.
J is for Janet who has jumped over a steeple.
K is for Kory who keeps a pet.
L is for Lewis who loves to bet.
M is for Matthew who munches chips.
N is for Naomi who nibbles people's lips.
O is for Oliver who opens doors.
P is for Polly who pushes apple cores.
Q is for Quentin who eats Quavers.
R is for Rebecca who rushes past erasers.
S is for Sophia who sucks dollies.
T is for Thomas who touches trollies
U is for Una who uses pencils.
V is for Vicky who visits stencils.
W is for William who wishes a lot.
X is for Xena who X-rays a pot.
Y is for Yama who yawns at goats.
Z is for Zack who zips coats.

Thomas Dunn (9)
Holne Chase Combined School

ALPHABET NAMES

A is for Ann who always eats apples.
B is for Ben who banks at Barclays.
C is for Chris who can break cans.
D is for Daniel who dumps dirty dishes.
E is for Emily who eats eggy eggs.
F is for Fred who fights flaming fires.
G is for Gertie who greets great Grandmas.
H is for Harry who hits hairy heads.
I is for Imran who's in inky places.
J is for Janet who jumps jammy jumps.
K is for Kory who counts kitty kittens.
L is for Lewis who loves licking lampposts.
M is for Matthew who munches millions of Marmite sandwiches.
N is for Naomi who never does as she's told.
O is for Oliver who opens doors to octopuses.
P is for Polly who pulls purple pigs.
Q is for Quentin who kisses the Queen.
R is for Rebecca who rushes all around.
S is for Sophie who likes salt and vinegar.
T is for Thomas who toots like a train.
U is for Una who uses everything.
V is for Victoria who visits vile vineyards.
W is for William who wraps everything up.
X is for Xena who X-rays, X-ray fish.
Y is for Yvonne who yodels on a yacht.
Z is for Zack who zips a lot of zips.

Matthew Carter (9)
Holne Chase Combined School

NAMES

A is for Annie Awkward who will never ever make up her mind.
B is for Bernard Barking, who is always shouting,
C is for Claire Colossal, who is extremely clever,
D is for David Diver who is swimming mad,
E is for Ellie Elegant, who is just so vain,
F is for Frederick Fever, who is always ill,
G is for George Gallops who is always wriggling,
H is for Humphrey Horn, who finds everything hilarious,
I is for Issy Inkwell who is always busy,
J is for Jack Jogger, who thinks he's so fit,
K is for Katherine Kollapser, who is always falling over,
L is for Lorna Luscious who is always eating cakes.
M is for Michael Marvellous, who is incredibly magnificent,
N is for Nina Nagger who is always nagging.
O is for Oliver Orchard who grows lots of apples.
P is for Penelope Parrot, who copies everyone she sees,
Q is for Quentin Quince who is always eating mince.
R is for Rachel Racherty who is always shaking.
S is for Sarah Singing who's in every choir you can think of.
T is for Tina Timer who is a world record racer.
U is for Ursula Universe who knows all about the stars.
V is for Vera Vacuum who's an excellent cleaner.
W is for William Walker who's got an incredible stride.
X is for X-ray X who knows his alphabet.
Y is for Yana Yoghurt who won't eat anything but yoghurts.
Z is for Zacchaeus Zoom who's a motorbike expert.

Amy Smith (9)
Holne Chase Combined School

THE RIVER'S JOURNEY

The trailing, rocky stream,
Bubbles gracefully and,
Tickles gently,
Like rain falling from the gloomy sky.

The noisy, splashy waterfall,
Falls bumpily and,
Scampers frantically,
Like a jogger galloping.

The swaying wide river,
Jiggles loosely and,
Sprays merrily,
Like a bowl full of jelly.

The stretching, relaxing ocean,
Laps quietly and,
Waves leaping,
Like a leaf blowing.

Simona Falconi (10)
Holne Chase Combined School

NOT JUST FOR CHRISTMAS

Brightly coloured wrapping paper,
Sleek and shiny bows,
A lid is lifted,
And a spirit is raised.

A playful paw bats at the air,
A slobbery tongue licks its bowl clean,
A cold wet nose sniffs the season,
And a happy bark is acknowledged.

Shrivelling paws tap an empty food bowl,
Big, crying eyes stare into nothingness,
A warm, dry nose sniffs the empty air sadly,
And the last whimper is heard, but ignored.

Jessica Harris (12)
Loughton Middle School

SPECTACULAR SPACE

I must go up to the stars again,
To the shining stars using wings.
I'll soar through space past the sparkling sun,
I'll do all of this in my dreams.

I must go up to the moon again,
To the magical moon using wings.
I'll manoeuvre round Mars to the mystical moon,
I'll do all of this in my dreams.

I must go up to the planets again
To the performing planets using wings.
I'll party round Pluto and prance playfully,
I'll do all of this in my dreams.

I must come back down to Earth again,
The extra-large Earth using my feet.
I'll enter the Earth with an ear-to-ear smile,
I'll do all of this when I wake.

Daniel Cashman (10)
Loughton Middle School

THE EVERLASTING SPIRIT

When you exist,
When you're alone,
When happiness sweeps over you,
It has always been there,
It always will be.

No one knows where it came from,
How it was given its name,
Is all lost without one?
It has always been there,
It always will be.

If you can't see it, how is it there?
What do you need it for?
What happens when you get separated?
It has always been there,
It always will be.

You're inactive without it,
The world a place from the past,
You'll see things you've never seen before,
Life will never last,
But. . . a spirit is everlasting.

Yasmin Jaffer (11)
Loughton Middle School

THE CREATURE

Beating drums and shouting voices echo through the night,
Flaming torches one by one fill the trees with light.
They chant and hum a cruel song the saddest ever made.
With guns in hand and blood-red meat they won't give up their raid.

But they are watched, by pale blue eyes filled with power and rage.
Why must *she* be sacrificed to fill this fashion change?
She is starving, stomach growling revealing her presence.
One head turns, then two, then three; let the chase commence.

Dashing through the undergrowth, sprinting through the trees.
Suddenly a searing pain shoots up from her knee.
Till her pain is stopped at last a rumbling purr.
Humans pull their knives and feel the quality of her fur.

Four young cubs, with tiny yowls, totter through the trees,
Seeing their mother lying bare one by one they freeze.
They go to her and together snuggle up in remaining fur.
Those pale blue eyes and clean white whiskers is all that remains of her.

Sarah Kellard (11)
Loughton Middle School

SCHOOL POEM

S chool every day of the week
C old on Mondays, don't want to get up
H ot or cold on Friday
O nly six weeks off at the most
O n the next we have one week off
L onely at play time no one to play with.

Timothy Batchelor (9)
New Bradwell Combined School

LIONS

Lions roaring loudly,
Jumping, pouncing their prey,
Dawn breaks, lions go for a drink
Evening comes, lions sleeping soundly.

Walking, daytime comes,
Yawning tired,
Hunting for food,
So tired, lazy, sleeping.

Alex Hosking (9)
New Bradwell Combined School

WINTER

Shivery,
Cold weather,
Snow is cold,
Icy,
Frost,
Freezing,
Snowflakes,
Snowy,
Watery.

Fiona Read (8)
New Bradwell Combined School

RECIPE FOR A CHILDREN'S PARTY

Take a supply of treats
And the presents
Add the children
With fun and laughter
Sprinkle the party poppers
Cakes and sweets
Cover with fun and joy
And then cut the cake
To remember when you're older.

Robert Erith (10)
New Bradwell Combined School

THE WEATHER

The weather can be tough.
The weather can be mean.
The weather can be wild.
The weather can be rough.

The weather can nip.
The weather can tear.
The weather can roar.
Like a lion.

The weather can be gentle.
The weather can be safe.

Jamie Simpson (8)
New Bradwell Combined School

THE WIND

The wind can be gentle.
The wind can be rough.
The wind can be soft
As a baby's skin

The wind can be calm
The wind can be angry
The wind can be hungry
Like a hungry bear.

Laura Richards (9)
New Bradwell Combined School

THE SUN!

The sun is rough.
The sun can be mad.
The sun is so angry
The sun is very hot.
The sun can be mean, so mean.
The sun can be wild.
The sun can *kill* you!
The sun is like a fireball.
The sun can be like an angry T-rex.

Kerry Felton (8)
New Bradwell Combined School

THE BEAR

The bear is brown,
The bear is rough,
The bear is wild,
The bear is angry,
The bear is soft,
The bear is hungry,
The bear is slow like,
The wind.

The bear is sleepy,
Like a rock,
The bear is mad,
The bear is wet,
The bear is dry like,
A leaf in the sky.

Kimberley Baker (8)
New Bradwell Combined School

CHOCOLATE

Chocolate can be white,
Chocolate can be black,
Chocolate can be yummy for your tummy,
I love chocolate, I love chocolate
Chocolate, chocolate, chocolate,
I love chocolate.

Anthony Thomas (8)
New Bradwell Combined School

THE BEAR

The bear is rough
The bear is tough
The bear is brown,
Browner than mud.
The bear is slow
The bear is angry
The bear is fast.
The bear is faster than me or a mouse.
The bear is calm,
The bear is furry.
The bear is a furry ball
It is fluffier than a car.

Joanne Packer (9)
New Bradwell Combined School

I LIKE TO ROAR, ROAR

I like to roar, roar,
All the time
In and out the house.
But my little sister says to me
'Growl, growl,'

I like to roar, roar
And growl.
But my little sister says to me.
'You will scare people so much.'

I like to
Thump, thump and roar.
Where I go.
But my little sister says to me
'Roar, roar and thump to me.'

Amy Bradley (8)
New Bradwell Combined School

THE BEACH

The sea is blue like a sky
The sand is like a sun
Bright and yellow
The rocks are grey, as the moon.

Michael Ereira (9)
New Bradwell Combined School

The Football Match

The match can be dirty,
The match can be clean,
The match can be as filthy
As a wrestling ring.

The match can be easy,
The match can be hard,
The match can be fast
Like you write a card.

The match can be tiring,
The match can be boring,
The match can be waiting
Just like Mum and Dad painting.

Tom Topping (9)
New Bradwell Combined School

UNCLE

Uncle is a bright orange,
He is a lumpy pillow,
Uncle is a loud bang,
He is a guide to a fun life.
Uncle is a warm fleece,
He is a running shoe.
Uncle is a roar from a lion,
He is the sun in summer.

Stephen Dachtler (10)
New Bradwell Combined School

COUNTING RHYME

One by one
One by one
Having fun doing my bun.

Two by two
Two by two
My mum is on the loo.

Three by three
Three by three
My name starts with a G.

Four by four
Four by four
I am poor.

Five by five
Five by five
A bee lives in a hive.

Six by six
Six by six
I pick up sticks.

Seven by seven
Seven by seven
I don't want to go to Heaven.

Eight by eight
Eight by eight
You are late.

Nine by nine
Nine by nine
I drink wine.

Ten by ten
Ten by ten
I saw a hen.

Gemma Bergman (8)
New Bradwell Combined School

COUNTING POEM

One by one
One by one
Now the song has just begun.

Two by two
Two by two
I had a trip to the zoo.

Three by three
Three by three
You have to climb a tree,

Four by four
Four by four
We saw a tramp and he was poor,

Five by five
Five by five
I'm not dead but I am alive.

Six by six
Six by six
Chop trees down and collect sticks.

Seven by seven
Seven by seven
If I had a holiday I would go to Devon.

Eight by eight
Eight by eight
Today I accidentally smashed a plate.

Nine by nine
Nine by nine
Today I committed a crime.

Ten by ten
Ten by ten
Tomorrow I'll be back again.

William Neal (8)
New Bradwell Combined School

AUNT

Aunt is a shocking pink
She is a high heel shoe
Aunt is a loud crash
She is a light from the sun
Aunt is a bright coat
She is a flaming hot pan
Aunt is a monkey hanging from a tree.

Shanon Smith (10)
New Bradwell Combined School

SLOWLY

As slowly as the baby crawls,
As slowly I will fall over a stool.

As slowly as my mum works,
Then slowly I will talk to her.

As slowly as I fall down the stairs,
As slowly as I see a bear.

As slowly as I call my sister,
As slowly as she pops her blister.

As slowly as the popcorn pops,
As slowly as this poem stops.

Kim Clare (11)
New Bradwell Combined School

JUNE

June is sliding lava
Blazing down,
A light as bright as
The burning sun.
A volcano ready
To explode.
A hot heater
Warming up.

David Yendell (10)
New Bradwell Combined School

RECIPE FOR A CHILDREN'S PARTY

Take a long hall,
And a few tables and chairs.
Add boys, girls,
Cupcakes and hot dogs.
Sprinkle with lights and music,
A DJ, games and competitions.
Cover with a scattering of decorations
And wrap in funny photographs
To look at by the fireplace.

Danielle Day (10)
New Bradwell Combined School

SLOWLY

Slowly the birds learn to fly.
Slowly the minutes tick by.
Slowly the sun rises to start a new day,
Slowly the cats creep away.
Slowly the branches of the trees sway and creak,
Slowly the man shuffles down the street.
Slowly the moon sneaks into view,
Slowly the birds drink all the dew,
Slowly we tiptoe downstairs,
Slowly the cat licks all its hairs.
Slowly the traffic trundles by,
Slowly the birds learn to fly.

Jane Iorizzo (11)
New Bradwell Combined School

THEME PARK RECIPE

Take a purse full of change
To wrap up the rain and add
Some sunshine
Add a little excitement
Mix some fun and laughter
Sprinkle a hint of bravery
To wrap up what has
Happened and put it in
My mind forever.

Sam Maude (11)
New Bradwell Combined School

AUNTIE

Auntie is a soft pink
She is as soft as a bed.
Auntie is a quiet one.
She is quite a chatterbox.
Auntie is as warm as a jumper is.
She is a cup of hot chocolate by
The fireplace.

Terrianne Higgs (10)
New Bradwell Combined School

RECIPE FOR A THEME PARK

Take a handful of rides
And a pinch of surprises.
Add shows and entertainment to
Sharpen up your life
With a scoop of amusements.
Sprinkle with a bundle of refreshments
Unless you bring a picnic.
Cover with bulky layers of excitement
And wrap it up with glorious photographs
To look at on boring days.

Ashley Whitmore (11)
New Bradwell Combined School

DAD

Dad is a green sporty colour
He is as warm as a bed cover
Dad is as soft as a pillow
He is as loud as a trumpet
Dad is a sleeping lion
He is spring sunshine.

Ryan Rowland (10)
New Bradwell Combined School

MUM

Mum is a smooth lilac
She is an actress with her eyes.
Mum is a distant shout.
She is a dipping slide.
Mum is a mohair jumper.
She is an early morning.
Mum is a chirpy budgie.
She is my mum.

Amy Dicks (11)
New Bradwell Combined School

DECEMBER

December is
A cloaked mist
Sent as cold as Christmas day
The snow spiders and icicles
Are on their way
The morning breeze
Crisp and deadly
The winter snow is falling
Heavily.

Lewis Smith (11)
New Bradwell Combined School

RECIPE POEM

Take a bag full of money.
And unwrap some sunshine.
Add a pinch of excitement,
With some friends.
Sprinkle on some fun and laughter,
And a hint of bravery.
Shake in something from the gift shop,
To remember on a wet and boring day.

Giles Brown (11)
New Bradwell Combined School

THE WIND

The wind is hard
The wind is cold
The wind is rough
The wind is hot
The wind is tough
The wind is strong
The wind is first
Like a rocket
The wind is light
The wind is ice
The wind is hard
The wind is soft
The wind is see-through
And I can't see the wind.

Kyle Frost (9)
New Bradwell Combined School

MY CAT LIKES TO HIDE IN BOXES

The cat from Japan looks like a man.
But my cat likes to hide in boxes.
The cat from the school jumped in the pool.
But my cat likes to hide in boxes.
The cat from my house likes to eat my mouse.
But my cat likes to hide in boxes.
The cat from London is called Amanda Blunden.
But my cat likes to hide in boxes.
The cat from China is a diner.
But my cat likes to hide in boxes.

Eleanor Pollard (8)
New Bradwell Combined School

MY ANIMAL POEM

The kissing spider is kissing in the castle.
The furry spider is funny on the fridge.
The bad spider is in the bath, bathing.
The strong spider is scary.
The lovely spider is looping into lollipop land.
The sweet spider is skipping in the sky.

Kerri Fennemore (8)
New Bradwell Combined School

MY FOOTBALL POEM

In the stand there are people cheering.
Cheering and cheering.
Around the players there are boots hitting the ground.
Squish and squash.
In the stand fans are shouting.
Screaming and screaming.

Joe Allen (8)
New Bradwell Combined School

MY SPIDER POEM

The hairy spider is hibernating.
The black spider is swinging.
The funny spider is fighting.
The happy spider hanging.

Daryl Roberts (8)
New Bradwell Combined School

MY CAT LIKES TO HIDE IN BOXES

My cat likes to hide in boxes.
The cat from Spain has a very big pain.
But my cat likes to hide in boxes.
The cat from Mexico likes to go to Texaco.
But my cat likes to hide in boxes.
The cat from the square likes to look like a bear.
But my cat likes to hide in boxes.
The cat from the school likes to jump into the pool.
But my cat likes to hide in boxes.

Robert Shacklock (8)
New Bradwell Combined School

MY CAT LIKES TO HIDE IN BOXES

The cat in the house likes to eat a mouse.
But my cat likes to hide in boxes.
The cat from London loves Amanda Blunden.
But my cat likes to hide in boxes.

Amanda Blunden (8)
New Bradwell Combined School

MY POEM

The fat spider was flying in the fire station.
The spotty spider was swimming in the sea.
The black spider was bouncing in the bouncy castle.
The lucky spider was very lucky and lived.
The cool spider was very cool and lived in a cool house.

Matthew Hill (8)
New Bradwell Combined School

MY CAT LIKES TO HIDE IN BOXES

The cat from the school likes the swimming pool.
But my cat likes to hide in boxes.
The cat from Japan looks like a man.
But my cat likes to hide in boxes.
The cat from my house likes to eat my mouse.
But my cat likes to hide in boxes.
The cat from London likes Amanda Blunden.
But my cat likes to hide in boxes.
The cat from France likes to dance.
But my cat likes to hide in boxes.

Catherine Amos (8)
New Bradwell Combined School

THE SPIDER

The smiling spider is spinning
The panting spider is paddling
The inky spider is interested
The dinky spider is dirty
The incey spider is escaping
The ramming spider is running.

Michael Iorizzo (8)
New Bradwell Combined School

MY WIND POEM

One day I woke up to the sound of wind.
Waving loudly.
The wind was rushing by the leaves.
Swirling dreadfully.
The wind was rustling the leaves.

Adana Roberts (8)
New Bradwell Combined School

MY SPIDER POEM

The tiny spider is in the tree.
The fat spider is flying in the hospital.
The lovely spider is going to go in the fire.
The swimming spider is drowning in the deep end of the pool.
The spider is going to the fire station.

Daniel Coll (8)
New Bradwell Combined School

MAN CALLED OOZE

There was an old man called Ooze,
Who drank a whole bottle of booze,
He fell down the stairs,
Falling over some pears,
Then ran away on a cruise.

Leanne Beard
New Bradwell Combined School

COOL SCHOOL

School, school,
Class school,
The cool guys rule,
The teachers aren't cruel.

School, school,
Pukka school,
What's a metre stick?
The cross-country team, are quick.

School, school,
Wicked school,
I love school,
School's so cool.

Alexander Rolfe (10)
New Bradwell Combined School

MUM

Mum is yellow,
She is as comfy as a pillow.
Mum is a chatterbox,
She is a path through a warm wood.
Mum is a warm hat,
She is a cup of soup by the fire.
Mum is a sleeping hamster,
She is summer sunshine.

Nicola Craig (11)
New Bradwell Combined School

BUZZY THE BEE

Buzzy the bee is busy
Buzzy the bee is angry
Buzzy the bee is funny
Buzzy the bee is silly
Buzzy the bee is daft
Buzzy the bee is foolish
Buzzy the bee is ridiculous
Buzzy the bee is senseless
Buzzy the bee is stupid
Buzzy the bee is amusing
Buzzy the bee is witty
Buzzy the bee is fussy
Buzzy the bee is black
Buzzy the bee is silky
Buzzy the bee is sleek
Buzzy the bee is smooth
Buzzy the bee is soft.

Sally Joyce Gray (10)
New Bradwell Combined School

SEASONS

S pring comes first,
E veryone enjoys the New Year,
A nd next is
S ummer and it's very hot
O ctober brings a frosty autumn and
N ext is winter, the coldest of the lot
S now, frost, cold and ice all comes with it.

Joe Sapwell (9)
New Bradwell Combined School

IN A CITY

In a city,
It is busy.
In a city,
It is noisy.
In a city,
Cars go by, buses stop.
In a city,
People rush around.
In a city,
The clock tower rings.
In a city,
Shop tills ring.
In a city,
People come and people go.

Charlotte Franklin (10)
New Bradwell Combined School

THOSE SCHOOLS DOUBLE Z'S MAKE UP WORDS

Razzle
Dazzle
Muzzle
Guzzle
Sizzle
Buzzle
Wazzle
Guzzle
Puzzle
Frizzle
Sozzle
Buzzy
That's the end of school.

Shelley Smith (9)
New Bradwell Combined School

SUMMER

Summer is hot
Summer is fun
People enjoy themselves on the beach
They make sandcastles,
Swim in the bright blue sea,
And run along the soft yellow sand.

James Wilson (9)
New Bradwell Combined School

HOT AND COLD

Cool man walking down ill lane,
Hot dude walking, walking on sunshine,
Cool man is as cool as ice,
Hot dude is hot like the sun,
What happens, happens when they meet?
Vapour and steam!

Lee Pilborough (10)
New Bradwell Combined School

WINTER

Winter is the coldest season,
On the eleventh month Guy Fawkes committed treason.
In the winter I dress up in warm clothes and my fingers freeze.
Sometimes when I am walking in the wind I,
Feel the breeze blowing in my face.

Aurie Jefferies (11)
New Bradwell Combined School

CAT POEM

My cat likes to play rugby,
A cat from next door likes to go shopping,
But my cat likes to play rugby,
A cat from Jamaica likes to be a maker,
But my cat likes to play rugby
Another cat from next door likes to draw,
But my cat likes to play rugby,
A cat from New Bradwell likes to work,
But my cat likes to play rugby.

Lyden Jefferies (8)
New Bradwell Combined School

CAT POEM

My cat likes to eat cat food,
A cat from France likes to dance,
But my cat likes to eat cat food,
A cat from China likes to eat in a diner,
But my cat likes to eat cat food,
A cat from next door likes to scream,
But my cat likes to eat cat food.

Charlie McLatchy (8)
New Bradwell Combined School

CANDLE POEM

Hot fire,
Blue dripping wax,
Scorching fire blazing,
From the black wick,
Flashes and smoke light,
Wax melts.

Connor Dale (8)
New Bradwell Combined School

CAT POEM

My cat likes to jump high
A cat from India wants to be an Indian.
But my cat likes to jump high
A cat from France likes to fish.
But my cat likes to jump high.
A cat from a playground likes to chase dogs.
But my cat likes to jump high.

Sophie Rowell (8)
New Bradwell Combined School

CANDLE POEM

Fire hurts
Dribbling gas
Flames are sources of light
See-through fire is a flame that can burn you
Wax melts.

Sam Camozzi-Jones (8)
New Bradwell Combined School

CAT POEM

My cat likes to eat cat food,
A cat from Spain
Likes the rain,
But my cat likes to eat cat food,
A cat from next door
Likes to dance,
But my cat likes to eat cat food,
A cat from India
Wants a hat,
But my cat likes to eat cat food,
A cat from France
Likes to sing,
But my cat likes to eat cat food,
A cat from Japan
Likes to sleep,
But my cat likes to eat cat food,
A cat from the garden
Likes to swim,
But my cat likes to eat cat food,
A cat from the farm
Likes bowls,
But my cat likes to eat cat food,
A cat from China
Likes spiders,
But my cat likes to eat cat food.

Charlotte Dunhill (8)
New Bradwell Combined School

CAT POEM

My cat likes to snore,
A cat from Spain likes to drive a crane,
But my cat likes to snore,
A cat from France likes to dance,
But my cat likes to snore,
A cat from Spain likes the rain,
But my cat likes to snore,
A cat from Bradwell likes to eat eggs,
But my cat likes to snore,
A cat from Japan likes to drive a van,
But my cat likes to snore,
A cat from Spain likes to drive a plane,
But my cat likes to snore,
A cat from France likes to dance,
But my cat likes to snore,
A cat from Jamaica likes to be a maker,
But my cat likes to snore.

Helen Dalgleish (8)
New Bradwell Combined School

SMELL

What is cooking?
I wonder,
I hope it's chicken,
Smells nice,
Great!
It's ready,
Delicious chicken,
This is nice.

Daniel Brooks (8)
New Bradwell Combined School

CAT POEM

My cat likes to fly,
A cat from Japan likes to play with a pan,
But my cat likes to fly,
A cat from Jamaica likes to dance,
But my cat likes to fly,
A cat from Spain sat on a train,
But my cat likes to fly.

Alice Taylor-Hodge (8)
New Bradwell Combined School

TAI FU WRATH OF THE TIGER

Tai Fu is a cool PlayStation game
Tai Fu is a male tiger all the same
He stands on his two back paws
And when he's annoyed he does roar
He also fights in Kung Fu style
And sends his enemies half a mile
Tai Fu rapidly kicks and punches
He kills foes in lethal bunches
He was trained by the Mantis Clan
Tai Fu's not afraid of any man
He defeated the leopards in their own home
And now he's gonna kill the dragon in his dome
Tai Fu is a friend of the drunk monkey king
And Tai Fu flies without a single wing
The last and final thing I will say
Is Tai Fu will get you, night or day.

Sean Keaney (11)
New Bradwell Combined School

SMARTY PARTY

There was a boy called Marty
He had an invitation to a party
Before he went, he went to buy some clothes
The colour he chose was mauve
Then he went to the party
And everybody called him Smarty.

Christopher Jennings (10)
New Bradwell Combined School

SLOWLY

Slowly the mouse awakes from his sleep,
Slowly the mole digs down very deep,
Slowly the bird flies round and round,
Slowly the squirrels crawl on the ground.

Slowly the wind twirls the leaves round,
Slowly the rain falls to the ground,
Slowly the ground begins to get wet,
Slowly the sun will soon set.

But what is slowest of all?
The night until the birds call.

Adam Weston (11)
New Bradwell Combined School

CANDLE POEM

Hot wax drips down flames,
Red dripping wax,
Red fire goes up,
Flashes and smoke balances light,
Wax melts.

Ashleigh Clements (8)
New Bradwell Combined School

BOATS

I walked upon a ferry,
I saw my friend Jerry,
Me and Jerry upon a ferry.
The swishing, swoshing from the water,

Rocked our boat.
The roaring engine made the boat float.
The end of tour one,
That was fun.
I and Jerry still waiting for the boat to go,
Jerry told sad stories,
And made me full of woe.

Joshua Pilborough (10)
New Bradwell Combined School

DRAGONS

D ragons raging
R aging dragons
A cross the sea
G aining on me
O n the way dragons go
N o one to be seen
S pin away.

R oaring flames
O h help me so
A mazing speed
R aining hard.
I n his cave
N eeding to come out
G rabbing me.

Jamie Gibbons (10)
New Bradwell Combined School

MY PUPPY LUCY

My puppy Lucy
Is rather naughty.
She nibbles my fingers and
Chews my toes.
When in the garden she
Chases the hose.
She wees on the floor
And scratches the door,
To let me know she wants
To go for an evening walk.
I love my puppy.
She's cuddly and sweet
She likes to lie across my feet.

Aimme Camozzi-Jones (11)
New Bradwell Combined School

THE WACKY ROMANS AND CELTS

All the Romans ran up the street
With leather sandals on their feet
The Celts were charging like mad
It looked like they were going to do something bad
They ended up in the middle
When suddenly Boudica jumped up playing a fiddle
They all danced and pranced around
Then they all fell to the ground
The Romans were in disarray
And just one step from running away
Up jumped Caesar
Offering a Malteser to Teresa
In the end the Romans won the day.

Nick Rixon (10)
New Bradwell Combined School

WHAT'S ON MY TEACHER'S DESK

T eacher's desk
E lastic bands,
A immes go-gos,
C ups of cold coffee,
H andful of tissues,
E mma's pen,
R egister messed up
S crunchies took from blare

D iary from two years ago,
E lephant statue,
S ellotape half used up,
K im's homework,
   That desk's a mess!

Lucy Johnson (10)
New Bradwell Combined School

THE NIGHT CAME DOWN

The night came down on the mice
As they scampered in the grass,
The night came down on the deer
As they slowly passed,

The night came down on the owls
As they flew down from tree to tree,
The night came down on the fox
As he was just to be free,

The night came down on the houses
Like a curtain falling down,
The night came down on the people
And now there isn't a sound.

Lydia Matthews (10)
New Bradwell Combined School

FLOWERS

F   lowers are colourful
L   ovely and bright
O   n my wall I have flowers
W   e play in the light
E   very flower I like is pretty
R   ain makes them grow
S   un makes them bright

Hannah Garrett (9)
New Bradwell Combined School

BOATS

B   oats rocking up and down,
O   ver the side splish, splosh, splash,
A   ll is silent except for splish, splash.
T   all boats, short boats they're all there
S   parkling and shimmering on the waves.

Spike Wyn-De-Bank (9)
New Bradwell Combined School

THE ABANDONED HOUSE

Feeling frightened, I gaze around the room,
Feeling frightened, I step and hear a *boom*!

Very scared, I ran up to my mum,
Very scared, I screamed and bit my thumb.

Terrified, I saw a Frankenstein,
Terrified, shivers went right the way, up my spine,
I hurried out the room.

Aaron Norman-Brown (10)
New Bradwell Combined School

I WILL TALK TO NAN TODAY

I will talk to Nan today Mum
I will talk to Nan ok
Can I just go out to play, Mum
Can I just go out to play?
I'll be back in a min, Mum
I'm just going away.

Naomi Holness (9)
New Bradwell Combined School

ART CLUB

Art club is good it is cool
Running to it after school
Turning corners running fast.

Class is empty I'm not last
Let's get down to doing some art
Under the roof of our school it is very, very cool.
But when we go home, I am sad. Then I see my grandad.

Ben Smith (11)
New Bradwell Combined School

ICE SKATING

Crash, crash goes the hockey sticks,
Crash, bash goes the hockey sticks
The player's heads bang
Bang goes the hockey sticks
They bash heads together
Bash, bash go their heads
When they tackle, then they crash
The player's skates go swish on the ice
The people cheered for men.

Alix Edwards (8)
New Bradwell Combined School

THE SUN

The sun is hot, hot, hot, hot.
The sun is mad.
The sun is as mad as a T-rex.
The sun is angry.
The sun is big and fat.
The sun can be mean.
The sun can be as mean as the Devil.

Jack Maude (8)
New Bradwell Combined School

THE WIND

The wind crashes against the haunted ship.
Moaning and whining to pirates on board.
Creaking as it's pushed into the jagged rocks of the cave.
Throwing itself against the ragged side of the ship.
Creaking and snapping when the mast breaks.
Pushing, shoving the boat up onto the shore.
Settling calming down very, very slowly as the sun sets.

Rosie Stevenson (10)
New Bradwell Combined School

SCHOOL

Playing is fun especially go-gos,
Dinner time's the best because
We have lots of nice food,
Play time is good for all,
The different things, play,
Games are brilliant for,
All the sports,
We do,
Class is okay my favourite,
Subjects,
Are history and geography,
Home time is the best of all.

Ryan Pollard (10)
New Bradwell Combined School

AUTUMN WINDS

When the autumn winds do come
The leaves go around and around
Until they fall and touch the ground.
When you see people walk on the
Lovely golden crispy leaves
All you hear is crunch, crunch, crunch.
When you see the leaves turn crispy
And brown. That's when you know
Autumn is here.

Frances Storey (11)
New Bradwell Combined School

THE SOLAR SYSTEM

Mercury's the nearest one,
Closest to our dazzling sun.
Venus is scorching hot,
Too much for our earthly lot.
Earth is where we all shall stay,
Every year and every day.
Mars is next and yes it's red,
Life over there was long ago dead.
Jupiter is nearly made of gas,
But it has by far the biggest mass.
Saturn is famous for its rings,
But we still need to discover many things.
Uranus is rarely seen,
Although it is an eccentric green
Neptune is near the back,
And the wettest of the pack.
Pluto is last and least,
For it is in our solar system, a little piece.
Comets, asteroids, stars and moons,
We could be exploring them very soon.

Jacob Sapwell (11)
New Bradwell Combined School

BROTHERS

Brothers, who needs them?
They never leave you alone
When you want to be on your own
Brothers, who needs them?
I try not to get angry at them I try my best
Brothers, who needs them?
Nevertheless I hit the annoying pests
Brothers, who needs them?
I try; I do try my best but with three
Of them it puts me to the test
The little *devils*

Jonathan Wilson (Age 11)
New Bradwell Combined School

FOOTBALL

When I play football, I sometimes score a goal
When I play football, I always trip and fall
When I'm watching football, they all have wicked shots,
I play football to reach the very top,
Football, football, that's my way,
I wish I could play for the best one day!

Jamie Walker (11)
New Bradwell Combined School

FLAME

Flame! The blinding, twinkling flickering hero.
Flame! The dazzling, flashy ruler of blazes.
Flame! With her gleaming, resplendent face,
Flame! With her lively colourful clothes,
Flame! The lurid, tawdry flaming master
Of the shiny fires.

Melissa Hill (11)
New Bradwell Combined School

FLAMING WITCH

Casting a spell on the big black cat.
Making potions with the big hairy bat.
Look at her nose it looks like both of her big toes.
Look at her spot it's sure to be bigger than that pot.
I have never seen such a cloak
I've got to say it looks like a bloke.

Leah Warren (10)
New Bradwell Combined School

ANIMALS

Animals jump and leap around
Ants dig underground
As leopards look up high
Monkeys swing in the trees
As they look beyond the seas.

Animals creep in the deep
As the crabs sweep
Baby fishes just been born
As the shore gets torn
Starfish in a rock pool
And the weather is very cool.

Eva Rice Leask (9)
New Bradwell Combined School

THOUGHTS

The sea slashes against the cliffs,
Angrily,
Like the brown lion,
Killing its prey.

The scarecrow stands in the dark damp field,
Lonely,
Like a ghost, sheet white,
In a haunted, house.

The birds fly and sing up in the clouds,
Beautiful,
Like a dolphin, swimming gracefully,
In a Caribbean Sea.

The hedgehog sleeps, in his nest of golden leaves,
Hidden,
Like a bat in his tree,
As the sun rises.

Annie Iorizzo (9)
New Bradwell Combined School

SCHOOL DAYS

Starting a day at school,
Continuous talking,
Hoping for the day to end,
Oh I hate school,
Oh it's so boring,
Lifting up your eyelids,

Drowsy in the sun,
After a long break,
Yawn, yawn, yawn,
Snore, snore, snore.

David Jones (10)
New Bradwell Combined School

TEACHERS HUMOURS

Helpful teachers
Giving you the answers
Playing games when you want
Making you good prancers
You can do what you want
Even quite high reaches

Old teachers
Giving you the creep
Telling you what to do
Standing there in a grumpy heap
Making you jump shouting '*boo*!'
They are beastly creatures

Funny teachers
Acting like a clown
Telling kids lots of jokes
Always wearing a pink and blue crown
Dressing up like Irish folks
They're becoming good preachers.

When you're going to a new school
Make sure you get a teacher that's nice
Or get driven up the wall by a
Curseful witch.

Barry Read (10)
New Bradwell Combined School

AUSTRALIA

Australia, with its flaming red-hot sun,
If I was you, you had better run,
Koala bears, kangaroos,
Boomerangs and didgeridoos.

Andrew Simpson (10)
New Bradwell Combined School

ROLLER COASTER

Round and round away we go I hope that
This will be slow.
Oh, no here we go we're going to crash!
We're lucky we didn't have a near bash.
Everybody with a scream and a shout
Now it's going to wobble about.
I close my eyes.
And I realise this is not scary.
When is this going to end?
Just one more bend.

Luke Tucker (10)
New Bradwell Combined School

DRAGON

D ark and damp is the cave where the dragon lives.
R ed-hot flames rush out of his mouth as he roars.
A ngrily he chases artists and any other men away.
G etting bigger every day, he growls grumpily.
O nly the brave would try to fight him.
N o one, not even, a knight has managed to defeat him.

Rebecca Dunhill (9)
New Bradwell Combined School

No Dog

No dog, oh no!
She was full of life!
She was as white as snow!

No dog, oh no!
I loved her so much!
Three woofs I would hear each morning!

No dog, oh no!
Her fur was silver in the moonlight!
All I thought was how pretty she was!

Oh no, no dog!

Katharine Sorrell (10)
New Bradwell Combined School

THE SEA

Roar, roar goes the engine.
Splash, splash go the choppy waves.
Sparkle, sparkle goes the gleaming sea.
Twinkle, twinkle go the fishes.
Sway, sway goes the boat on the sea.

David Gee (9)
New Bradwell Combined School

BOAT RIDE

The waves slapping against my side,
As I rage through the wide, tide for this is a bad ride,
The waves are flying up beside me,
As the water gives way to the boat.
The roaring engine pushing waves along its side
As the hurling and curling wave splashed
And no one *behaved*!

Robert Hayle (9)
New Bradwell Combined School

THE WAVES

I was outside of a boat,
The waves were all whacking the sides,
When I was speeding up the boat,
All the waves came up and were roaring,
They also came up smelling, up out of the water,
They were sploshing under the bottom,
The boat tremendously was swaying up above,
The waves were all rocking,
They were wavy and gigantic waves,
They were splendid and quietly fantastic.

Jack Hamilton Snell (9)
New Bradwell Combined School

KITTENS

Kittens are playful.
Kittens are cute.
Dashing and splashing wears them out.
So put them to bed in a nice warm place.
They will be back putting smiles on your face.

Laura Reeve (10)
New Bradwell Combined School

As The Water Rocks And Waves

As the water starts to wave,
Side by side,
As the boat waves and rocks,
Side by side
As the speed boats zoom by,
The boats rock,
Side by side
The fish jump up and down,
Little twinkles fade away.
Watching the fishermen catch fish,
Struggling.

Jordan Green (10)
New Bradwell Combined School

THE SEA

As you hit a wave
It looks dazzling and sparkling
Splash! As you drop something
Chop! Chop! Chop!

Look sharp; see the big fish,
Don't disturb,
Sail away.

Daniel Feasey (9)
New Bradwell Combined School

BLOWING IN THE WIND

They are blowing in the wind
Owl that fell down in the wind,
Down, down, down in the wind,
Why did the frog jump up in the wind?
Why, why, why did it jump up in the wind?

Darrell Chapman (10)
New Bradwell Combined School

DASHING AND SPLASHING

The raging engine dashing and splashing as I go
Twinkling ripples overlapping.
One gigantic wooden wheel slapping on the water
Steam, rushing and gushing out of me
I am going up and down a gigantic deep lake.
Splash, splash splash
Dash, dash dash.
Jump I hit the bank
Everybody rushing off
Everybody rushing on.
The raging engine dashing and splashing
As I go.

Callum English (10)
New Bradwell Combined School

UP SO HIGH IN THE SKY

Up so high in the sky
Lays two rainbows side by side
Above the rainbows stood a volcano
Rumbling away like breadcrumbs
I stood and watched the rainbow
It had loads of bright colours like the stars at night.
The volcano was red with brown round the edge.

Lucy Pearson (10)
New Bradwell Combined School

THE BATTLE

The two ancient enemies looked at each other,
Each facing the other under the black sky.
A wizard, a demon – two ancient brothers,
The winner would rule, the loser would die.

The creature was first – its steel claws flashing.
He lunged to the neck of the warrior-priest.
The sorcerer leaped, avoiding the slashing.
He prepared a defence to vanquish the beast.

Screaming a word, he called forth the lightning,
Striking his foe with a bolt from the blue.
But calling on new life the monster rose, brightening.
Smiting his enemy, raging, renewed.

And with a vicious roaring firestorm,
The being then attacked.
Being a Child of Fire, the hellspawn just felt warm.
But the image fell, his skull cracked.

Conagh Laslett (9)
New Bradwell Combined School

THE SEASIDE

Today we're going to the seaside,
The sand sparkling white,
Look you see the sea.
With waves twinkling high.

You see the sandcastle.
Holes that are
The sunbathers burn, with balls flying everywhere
When you go past the seagulls you can hear them go cheep.

At night-time there are sparkling lights.
Which glitter through the night
You want to stay there for long hours,
You finally do, it's morning now, the lights are out it's time to go.

Victoria Johnston (10)
New Bradwell Combined School

I Don't Like . . .

I don't like burgers
I don't like beans
I don't like custard
I don't like cream
I don't like cabbage
I don't like stew
I don't like gravy
I don't like glue
I don't like pasta
I don't like chips
I don't like sausages
I don't like dips
I don't like treacle
I don't like goo
I don't like anything cooked by you

Leigh Taylor (10)
New Bradwell Combined School

MY BEST FRIEND

My best friend was a dog,
It was black and white,
It didn't write with its left,
It didn't write with its right,
Its tongue was pink,
Its eyes were red,
Its nose was wet and black,
It was my best friend
Called Tosh.

Molly Gibbs (10)
New Bradwell Combined School

FOOD!

Wet food,
Mushy food,
Hot food,
Slushy food,
Cold food,
Green food,
Dry food,
Clean food,
Takeaway food,
Weird food,
Cooked food,
Smeared food,
Mouldy food,
Fat food,
Fast food,
Cat food,
Smelly food,
Mashed food,
Lumpy food,
Bashed food,
Sweet food,
Minty food,
Square food,
Wrinkly food.

Christian McPherson (10)
New Bradwell Combined School

WAR

'We are at war with Germany'
This is what started it . . .
Bang! Boom! Bang!
What was that?
Kaboom!
Aah!
Bombs dropping,
Planes flying,
Dead people everywhere,
AA guns firing
Messerschmidts everywhere
Spitfires . . *Bang!*
Hurricanes . . .*boom*!
Blitzed houses
Buzz . . .
Doodlebug! . . . 3 2 1. . .
Boom!
. . . *Boom*!
V2!
What's that noise?
A crowd up there buying rations?
No!
A crowd celebrating!
Hitler's dead. . .
Whistle while you work,
Hitler is a jerk,
He and his army drive me barmy,
Whistle while you work.

Scott Whitmore (9)
New Bradwell Combined School

ADVENTURE

A dventure,

D on't go on one unless you are prepared they can be,

V iolent, inspiring, cool and amazing,

E veryone wants to go on one but,

N obody has ever dared.

T here are plenty of,

U ntoward things that could happen,

R unning out of food and equipment,

E verybody wants to experience the adventure.

Moss Bancroft (9)
New Bradwell Combined School

DON'T EAT WITH YOUR MOUTH OPEN

'Don't eat with your mouth open,'
Said my father.
It just wasn't fair,
My brother had his mouth open,
And was also croakin'
My dad sat down and drank his tea,
While I just stared,
At my peas.
Then I spat at my brother
My dad went out and told my mother
My mum came in and said
'You get upstairs to bed'
D'oh!

Michael Dicks (9)
New Bradwell Combined School

ROCKETS

1 2 3 off it goes up so high,
Will it reach the sky? It goes fast,
Faster than a cheetah. Oh look its reached space.
4 5 6 It's came down on the lander, everybody is
Pleased. They're on TV! Rockets popular everybody likes it
Oh look there off again. Will they make it back? Yes they
Do, they brought photos back there in the museum and their
Suits. Their rocket is on show.

Victoria Johnson (9)
New Bradwell Combined School

THE BEACH

The beach is fun.
When the weather is warm.
The sun shines on the water.
It's cold when it touches your feet.
People swimming in the sea.
Looking as happy as can be.

Callum Astrella (9)
New Bradwell Combined School

STARS

S   tars, there are so many
T   winkling in the sky
A   re there living things up there?
R   ockets flying to the moon
S   till at night I lie down looking at the stars.

Thomas Lepelaars (10)
New Bradwell Combined School

INTERNET

I   love surfing the
N   et. The games,
T   he music and quizzes are so
E   njoyable.
R   eceiving
N   otes and
E   mail from my friends and
T   elling them about the fun I have on the *Internet.*

Marguerite Willett (10)
St Mary & St Giles CE Middle School

BEST MATES

They play together every day
They're good mates in every way
But everyone has beginnings and ends,
Even when they're best friends.
One of them refused to play,
So Wednesday they fell away.
Now they play together every day.
They're good mates in every way.

Dominic Bush (10)
St Mary & St Giles CE Middle School

THIS WEEK'S TIMETABLE

On Monday I went out to play,
On Tuesday I went to my grans to stay.
On Wednesday I went out to lunch,
On Thursday I ate a packet of crisps with a big
Crunch!
On Friday I did a test,
On Saturday I took a rest.
On Sunday I was on the plane,
The week started all over again.

Tasmina Begum (11)
St Mary & St Giles CE Middle School

SCHOOL'S UP!

Down in the playground
It's a freeze up, sneeze up
Waiting for the bell.
Then off in line
Where it's a squeeze up,
Tease up no more shout and yell.
But very soon
It's a knees up, wheeze up
PE in the hall.
Followed by a cheese up,
Please up dinner time call.
Then afternoon and busy bees up,
Seize up when all work's done.
Until it's ease up,
Tea's up so it's home time . . .
Run!

Sara Kerpel (9)
St Mary & St Giles CE Middle School

MY DOG

My dog chases her tail,
No matter how hard she tries she always fails,
She's black, white and ginger too,
She's very naughty when she chews my dad's shoe,
Every day she runs around the house,
Sometimes I wish she was as quiet as a mouse,
She's got big pointy ears and a long nose,
You cannot blame no one else when she gets wet when she
Chases the hose,
She comes running up to me when I get home from school,
But I think my dog's really, really cool.

Amber Neal (10)
St Mary & St Giles CE Middle School

I WISH

I wish everybody had good friends.
I wish all the TVs could bend.

I wish there were more fun schools.
I wish every house had swimming pools.

I wish we had free holiday flights.
I wish we had electronic kites.

I wish people wouldn't die.
I wish we had lots of pie.

I wish we had free cool cars.
I wish we went to Mars.

I wish we had lots of money.
I wish people would be more funny.

I wish there was lots of snow
I wish turtles wouldn't go slow.

I wish we had Christmas everyday
I wish we didn't have to pay.

I wish, I wish, I wish.

Poonam Sampat (10)
St Mary & St Giles CE Middle School

MY FAMILY

He's big and funny
And married to Mummy
That's my dad.

She's pretty and kind
The best you can find
That's my mum.

He laughs and he's crazy
A little bit lazy
That's my Jordan.

He's cuddly and sweet
But has smelly feet
That's my Saul.

Last but not least
Eats like a beast
That is me.

We had some fun
As you've met each one
That's my family!

Zara Turvey (9)
St Mary & St Giles CE Middle School

SPACE

Dancing comets, shooting stars
Aliens zooming round in cars
Whirling little galaxies singing in the night
Shooting planets all in a fright
Tiny disco dancers getting really late
Pink plimps from Pluto gathering up lots of bait.

Tess Öner (8)
St Mary & St Giles CE Middle School

DREAMING

I dream of
Chocolate that
Will last forever
You never go to
School ever
I live in a mansion
With a swimming
Pool
My dream may
Come true.

Corinna Purnell (10)
St Mary & St Giles CE Middle School

MY DOG SONNIE

My dog Sonnie is my best friend
He plays with me for the rest of the day
He licks me when I give him a treat and
Most of all he is my best friend still.

My dog Sonnie is my best friend
My friends have seen him loads of times.
But he is still my best friend but the
One thing is I love him.

My dog is huge as can be,
He is hungrier than a baby.
But he is still my best friend
I love my dog Sonnie.

Robyn Coley (9)
St Mary & St Giles CE Middle School

MY BROTHER JOE

My brother's name is Joe.
And he watches Po.
His walls are pine.
And he is nine.
Joe likes pop.
And he wants to be a cop.
Joe grows corn.
And he has a lawn.

Martin Simm (10)
St Mary & St Giles CE Middle School

THE WITCH'S SPELL

Grubble, grubble, lots of trouble
Roaring fire make it bubble

Fill it with a crocodile
Add a bathroom's broken tile

Lizard's tongue and spoon that's bent
Wild honey and rusty tent.

Old lady who can't walk
Smelly sock, blackboard chalk.

Tail of a bear, ear of cat
Leg of fly, wing of bat

Grubble, grubble lots of trouble
Roaring fire make it bubble

Haroon Ahmed (10)
St Mary & St Giles CE Middle School

MY PUPPY HANNAH

My puppy Hannah,
She chews and chews her bone,
She drinks all her water,
She gets her nose all wet,
She's definitely my favourite pet.
Her food doesn't smell nice
But she eats it very quick
And then she has a drink
That's my puppy Hannah

Alice Hunter (9)
St Mary & St Giles CE Middle School

TREE

There once was a tree by our garden wall,
With great branches spreading out, proud and tall,
But now no longer proud and tall,
It lights our house and warms our hall.

In bygone summers I used to climb,
That wondrous tree, I called it mine,
But now no longer proud and tall,
It lights our house and warms our hall.

When it fell, fell crashing to the ground,
It made a frightening, smashing sound,
So now no longer proud or tall,
It lights our house and warms our hall.

So Dad got out his saw, hammer and axe,
Chopped the tree and put it in sacks,
So now no longer mighty and tall,
It lights our house and warms our hall.

Helen Miles (11)
St Mary & St Giles CE Middle School

ALIEN WORLD

In a land far away.
People got carried away.
Because a King called Anaway
Was telling them what to do.
They got fed up with him.
So they did their own *thing*.
They flew down to Earth
And gave birth
And they started a new alien
World.

Richard Ludbrook (10)
St Mary & St Giles CE Middle School

A FROG

Sitting on a lily pad all day long,
Having food and drink,
Did you see us humans
Washing in the sink?
Why do you just sit and stare,
Looking very sad why don't you
Come and play without your mum
And dad? Oh please don't run
Away, you have all the time to
Play. Why don't you come inside
So you will be by my side?

Rebecca Wade (10)
St Mary & St Giles CE Middle School

THE DENTIST'S CHAIR

I was at the dentist's – fair and square
Thinking about his big black chair
Moments later I got called in
There was the room, dark and dim
Then he turned on a light and it really gave me quite a fright.
Sitting there big and bright was a chair –
But not one that was there to scare.

Bethaney Price (10)
St Mary & St Giles CE Middle School

SNOWFLAKE POEM

Glinting snowy shapes.
Maybe it could hit your hair.
Making you feel cold.
Swirling, twirling round and round.
Heading towards the white ground.

Sarah Dutton (10)
St Mary & St Giles CE Middle School

THE OWL

The owl hoots, the owl swoops, silently through the night
He flutters his wings with such grace, at such an even pace,
His brown and golden chest is soft to touch and feel
He gazes into the night searching for his next meal
His head he turns the whole way round
Making sure he never misses a single sound.

Jessica Craft (10)
St Mary & St Giles CE Middle School

DREAM ISLAND

Walk on white sand,
On my favourite island,
Volcanoes towering over me,
While watching silver fish swim in the sea.

Seeing the lava rock landscape,
It is a place that you would not
Want to escape,
While watching tiny lizards scurry
No one is ever in a hurry.

Large sculptures watching as you go past,
Wishing this holiday would always last,
Sadly it's time to fly away,
But I will come back again someday.

Teddy Clifford (10)
St Mary & St Giles CE Middle School

OUR FINGERPRINTS

The prints we leave are everywhere
For years the walls will always wear

When morning comes again they show
Both near and far and high and low

On walls, TVs and tiled floors
On mirrors, glass and bathroom doors

Our fingerprints are on CDs
And on the screens of our TVs.

Dale Johns (9)
St Mary & St Giles CE Middle School

MIRROR

See your face on the wall
Hanging up in the hall
I cannot reach it I'll get a stool
I think I'm about to fall!

I give a shout! I give a scream
Suddenly I'm in a dream
What is it that I've just seen?
A guinea pig looks back at me

I open my eyes I'm all alone
Then I hear a funny groan
A little voice says 'Welcome home'
It's Scruffy my guinea pig on the phone.

Harriet Jones (9)
St Mary & St Giles CE Middle School

ME AND MY FRIEND

My name is Gemma,
And my friend is called Emma,
We play in the playground,
And we make a lot of sound,
We are in the cross-country squad,
And we're like peas in a pod,
We never fight,
And we never leave each other's sight,
Our friendship was right from the start,
And we will never be broken apart.

Gemma Brown (10)
St Mary & St Giles CE Middle School

DOLPHINS

D olphins are my favourite animals.
O ther fish are just mammals
L ooping, splashing, not to be found.
P erhaps I'll see one splashing around.
H ope they aren't stuck on the ground.
I love dolphins they're the best.
N ow, dolphins are better than the rest.
S o if you see a dolphin don't forget to tell me.

Jocelyn Hooley (9)
St Mary & St Giles CE Middle School

ONCE I TRAVELLED TO ANOTHER WORLD

Once I travelled to another world
The land there was rather pearled
All the people were very nice
I decided to eat them with rice.

Then I bought a chocolate drink
They said it would help me think
I said 'Sorry about that'
Then I bought them all a red hat

Andrew Carmichael (10)
St Mary & St Giles CE Middle School

THE JOURNEY

I got in the car for the journey
We travelled miles and miles
But when we got there
Our boot was bare

My grandma said let's unpack
But we told her the bags were at home
She let out a loud groan
So we made a return journey home.

Charlotte Spenceley (9)
St Mary & St Giles CE Middle School

TOMORROW

Tomorrow I might find
A friend
Tomorrow I might find
A pet
Tomorrow what will
Happen?
Tomorrow, tomorrow
What about
Tomorrow?

Natalie Loft (10)
St Mary & St Giles CE Middle School

I THINK MY BROTHER'S AN ALIEN

I think my brother's an alien,
And comes from outer space.
He's rubbish at his schoolwork,
And his hair's an utter digrace.

I think my brother's an alien,
And comes from planet Mars.
He doesn't watch any TV,
But he likes to study the stars.

Then one night I heard him say,
'I want to go home now.'
Then out of the darkness he saw something,
Which made him shout out, 'Wow.'

For he saw his planet Mars,
Coming nearer and nearer to him.
Then from that planet leapt someone,
And that someone's name was Jim.

My brother cried, 'Oh Jim, oh mate, oh Jim my only pal.
Why did you do it? Why did you leave me? Why oh why and how?'
Jim just smiled and looked around, then took my brother's hand.
Then he leapt lightly and quickly off the darkening land.

Then suddenly the planet Mars,
Shot off through a galaxy of stars.
And that's how my brother went to space,
But I bet his hair's still an utter disgrace.

Sarah Matthews (10)
St Mary & St Giles CE Middle School

I FEEL SICK!

I feel sick when I travel by sea, and one day I swear I
Will be.
I feel sick when I travel by plane, and I never want to do
It again!
I don't feel as sick when I travel by car, across the
Country, far and far.
But I get really grumpy when the seats get all
Lumpy travelling in the car.

Ciara Williams (10)
St Mary & St Giles CE Middle School

WINTER WIND

Winter wind blowing strong
Up above the winter sun
Winter wind cold all day
Winter wind here to stay
Winter wind here today

Stevie Loft (9)
St Mary & St Giles CE Middle School

MY LIFE

I love my mummy
My mummy loves me
We live together
As a family

I go to school
And try my best
We have lessons in maths
Then tables test

I train as a gymnast
On the floor, vault and beam
I've won some medals
Which was my dream.

Laura Smyth (9)
St Mary & St Giles CE Middle School

MY WISH CAME TRUE

I wish that I could sail a boat
Upon the sea so blue.
The wind apounding on my face
And on the great sails too.

Then I learnt to do just that
And I knew what I must do.
I had to have a big brown boat
With sails a lovely blue.

As we sailed away from shore
And out in the big blue sea.
Nothing would come close to how
I felt and the feeling of being so free.

Then when the day was almost through
I'd stay a while to see.
The sunset in the sky, the sea
And you and me.

Jenna Frost (11)
St Mary & St Giles CE Middle School

CAR CHASE

Swerve, swerve skid, skid
Don't bump into that little kid

Oh God I see the police
Quickly step on it fast Reece

It's happening help I see a stinger
I hate those things to the tips of my fingers

Quick, quick, open the door
And get the loot from the jewellery store

Oh my God they've got a gun
Quickly you lot now run

God I've tripped over a stone
I think I've broken all of my bones

Worse luck I'm held at gunpoint
Please don't drag me up my legs are at numb point

Boom, boom bang, bang
Why do I have to share a cell with a crazy axe man?

Christian Kemp (10)
St Mary & St Giles CE Middle School

KITTY

Whiskers twitched, tail shook
I stopped to take a second look.
In surprise he stared at me,
That's when I began to worry.
I saw a mouse as scared as could be,
Peeking out from under the tree
Kitty pounced, scratched and bit,
I shouted at him *'You cruel little boy!'*
But then I saw that it was only a toy.

Olivia Howarth (10)
St Mary & St Giles CE Middle School

CHEETAHS

I like cheetahs
They are meat eaters
They love to pounce and purr

They leap through the air
Run fast everywhere
And have big black spots on their fur.

Natasha Gilliland (8)
St Mary & St Giles CE Middle School

PEEK CREEK

Peek Creek
Is a spooky house,
With windows boarded
And the sound of a mouse.
Once inside,
In front of you there,
Floating and grinning,
On the topmost stair,
A ghost!
He slides down the banisters with a *whoosh*.
Gliding and sliding
He gives me a push.
I stumble and fall
And give a little shriek
I now know I'm bound
To haunt Peek Creek.

Debbie Claxton (10)
St Mary & St Giles CE Middle School

MY TEACHER IS AN ALIEN

My teacher is an alien
She used to live on Mars
She spends all her spare time eating milky bars.

She has eyes at the back of her head
And ears all over her face
She scribbles all over our work when it's wrong
And makes it a big disgrace.

The head is always on her,
Shouting and telling her off
She always gets things wrong and once ate the pet school moth.

My teacher is an alien
She used to live on Mars
She spends all her spare time eating milky bars.

Alice Frost (9)
St Mary & St Giles CE Middle School

BEDBUG!

'Mum,' I said one night.
'I'm scared of something could you turn on the light'
'What is it dear?'
Said Mum with no fear.
'It's a bedbug!' I cried!
'Silly child you have lied!'
I put my knees up to my head
And I jumped out of bed
I screamed, 'Hey! Hey! Hey!'
As my bed was walking away.

Emma Mosley (10)
St Mary & St Giles CE Middle School

MY BEST FRIEND

'My best friend is thoughtful.'
'My best friend eats chocolate!'
'My best friend is helpful.'
'My best friend can do a cartwheel!'
'My best friend thinks of others.'
'My best friend has lots of toys!'
'My best friend listens to me.'
'My best friend is better than yours!'
'Stop it! Stop it! Stop talking about your friend.
She's no friend of yours!'

Naomi Keogh (10)
St Mary & St Giles CE Middle School

THE RIVER RACES

It moves slowly,
It sways quietly,
It starts to run,
It began to fall,
The stream is roaring,
When it splashes,
More splashes come,
It starts sploshing,
It's falling down between the rocks,
And now it's splicing,
Small waves are racing,
All the way down the hill.

Natasha Perkins (10)
St Thomas Aquinas School

MY TROLL TIARA

I have a friend troll
Tiara is her name
We have lots of fun
Playing lots of games.

She has big blue hair
And a long pink dress
Compared to me
I look a right mess.

I'll style her hair for hours and hours
We do our make-up
We like to stay up all night long
Then we sing our song.

Then one day she came to me
And said 'I have to go away.
I just come to see you lived happily.'

I cried and cried
I could have died
But then I knew she loved me
And I would live happily.

Jennie Collins (10)
St Thomas Aquinas School

SCHOOL DINNERS

Spotty dick is really sick,
As well as mushy peas,
Try the mashed potato
It's hard like your knees.

The beans are like rocks,
The milk is always off.
The veg is really mushy,
Especially in the broth!

Elisha Martin (10)
St Thomas Aquinas School

MY OWN THOUGHTS OF A RIVER

My river is called Roger,
He's nowhere near an old codger.
He runs, he trickles,
He flows gently and when you touch him he tickles.
He sounds amazing; you will never have heard anything
                                            like this before,
And when you do a big splash he lets out an almighty *roar*!

He's sort of greeny blue,
You never know one in-between the two!
Sometimes if you just sit and listen he will begin to talk,
He will tell you about when he used to be able to walk.

If you look he will sparkle in your eyes,
When he's in the air it looks like he flies.
It's like he's looking back at me,
Or is he staring at the bee, which is flying around next to me!
He gets agitated when he's angry,
His every mood moves me.

Lucy Sullivan (11)
St Thomas Aquinas School

OUTER SPACE

Have you ever wondered?
What it's like in space.
Spacemen have thundered,
It's like they were having a race.
But that's not the best of it,
Cool flying saucers too.
Every little bit is like a virtual zoo.

All the little stars,
Twinkling in the sky.
There like little angels,
Waving and saying 'Hi!'
How I wish to be,
High up in the sky,
With those little wizards,
Right up really high.

Daniel Coyle (11)
St Thomas Aquinas School

THE BOYS BAD DAY

Look over there,
The boys in despair.
He can't work in here,
He can't work out there.

A bad day he's having,
A worse day than I'm having!
What can he do?
Maybe he could ask Doctor Who.

In maths he was rubbish,
In English, he wrote French!
In chemistry he tried,
But only managed to blow up the teacher!

It's three o'clock,
The bell starts ringing.
Just remember the boy,
Who had a bad day!

Paul Maxey (11)
St Thomas Aquinas School

FOOTBALL

Football is so much skill
So be a man and show it all
The best sport in the world is football
Score a goal and foul a player
Don't daydream like Alan Shearer
I play for Waterhall
We play like Liverpool
We never lose, not even to Man United
I always take the penalty
And I always miss
So let me score a penalty
Or I'll miss again.

Joseph Sullivan (10)
St Thomas Aquinas School

MY BEST FRIEND

My best friend is called Hannah,
She's not much bigger than a 10-inch spanner.

She's wild and lively,
Messy 'sometimes' tidy.

She's been my best friend for 9 years,
There's been laughter and a 'few' tears.

She has a wicked sense of humour,
She's more of a friend than you are.

She's my best friend,
So that's the end.

Katy Werboweckyj (10)
St Thomas Aquinas School

MY FAIRY

I believe in fairies
Some people don't,
I always look for fairies
But some people won't.

A fairy dies nearly every day
By the silly people that say
'I don't believe in fairies
And I never will,
I didn't as a baby and I
Don't still.'

One day when I was in the kitchen
I looked out on the garden wall,
I saw something very pretty,
But also very small.

'My name is Rosebud Mary' it said
'And guess what I'm a fairy
I find flowers very pretty and
Cats a little scary!'

'Lucy' I cried 'Lucy come quick'
Lucy was at my side in a tick,
'What is it you sound like somebody's died'
'No it's a fairy, a fairy' I cried.

'I don't believe in fairies' she said
'And I never will,
I didn't believe as a baby and I don't still!'

As I looked outside my fairy
Fell from the wall,
And a cat jumped over the wall
And quickly ate her all.

Ciara Callaghan (10)
St Thomas Aquinas School

ONE OLD MAN

Once lived an old man
He drove an old van
He drove his old van for money
He was saving up for an old monkey
He went to his old bank
To get out the money for the old monkey
He wanted the old monkey to clean up his old van
But the old monkey drove away
In the old van leaving the old man behind.

Isla Peters (11)
St Thomas Aquinas School

UNCLE'S BRAINS!

Uncle, his inventive brains,
Keep involving aeroplanes,
Fell from an enormous height,
On my garden lawn last night.
Flying is a faithful sport,
Uncle wrecked the tennis court.

Song

Uncle's inventions,
Can he fix them?
Uncle's inventions,
No he can't!

Sometime later, he did another one,
It really wasn't good at all,
That he blew it with his gun.

Jason D'Mello (11)
St Thomas Aquinas School

PIGGINS 2

Now that *'piggin Christmas'* is over,
And also the New Year,
We start thinking of *'piggin holidays,'*
That fills us all with *'piggin cheer.'*

Where shall we go?
I know!
'Piggin touring.'
All the *'piggin shopping'*
Will be *'piggin gorgeous,'*
That will make us *'piggin smile.'*
But also *'piggin guilty.'*
And make us think when we get home at last-*'piggin skint!'*

Never mind.
Lets have a *'piggin tea break,'*
I feel so *'piggin tired,'*
We'll take our tea and cakes
Out in the *'piggin garden,'*
And make out we're *'piggin retired.'*

Oh no!! Here come the *'piggin wasps!'*

Jennifer Lavender (10)
St Thomas Aquinas School

196